Python Mastery

A 'Code like a Pro' Guide for
Python Beginners

Jonathan Bates

CONTENTS

Introduction

1 What is Python?   1

2 Why Learn Python   4

3 Getting Started with Installation   7

4 Starting Techniques   11

5 Important Techniques and Strategies   15

6 Glossary   36

7 Conclusion   51

INTRODUCTION

I want to thank you and congratulate you for downloading the book, "Python Mastery: A code like a pro guide for python beginners"!

This book contains helpful steps and strategies on how to successfully use and manage this free programming language tool. This is made to be an interactive tutorial and guide in mind, so you can code on Python what you read here.

Programming is not a walk in the park. It requires a lot of patience, diligence, and understanding, with a bit of logical thinking from time to time. The high end programming for geniuses, but this ebook will help you get on the right track.

Thanks again for downloading this book, I hope you enjoy it?

1 WHAT IS PYTHON?

Python is a high-leveled, very useful and all-purpose programming language tool, named after a large, heavy-bodied, non-poisonous constrictor snake. Python has nothing to do with snakes or reptiles, unless you want to make a code about snakes, but that's getting ahead of ourselves.

Python is freely available and makes finding the solution to a computer problem just as simple as if you had written out your thoughts on how to find the solution. Python can be run on almost any computer without needing to change the program once the program is written.

Programming Languages

You have probably heard or seen programs like Java, JavaScript and C around, have you not? These are also programming languages. Programming languages are what allow programmers to develop software programs, scripts, and instructions for computers to follow.

There are a LOT more programming languages than those I have listed here, and some have very specific focus. Programming language can be used for different fields of programming, as listed down here:

1. Application and Program Development: these involve programs you work with on daily. For example, an Internet browser program you use to view your favorite pages, or an

app that allows you read ebooks such as this on your kindle, are examples of programs made this way.

2. Artificial Intelligence Development: this is dedicated to making AIs, or cognitive systems, that can interact with human behavior and learn. Programs made here include character interactions on computer games, parts of programs that make decisions, and chatboxes that can reply back to the sender.

3. Database Development: self-explanatory: you make and maintain mini-databases, which hold large quantities of digital information for people to look up and use. These are important for websites to have so they can compile information.

4. Game Development: also self-explanatory: Computer games and other entertainment software can be written by language programs like Java (and flash games you can find online use that same script).

5. Computer Drivers or other hardware interface development: programs made with this focus in mind support hardware functionality.

6. Internet and Web Page Development: The lifeblood of the Internet. Without developers, there could be no web pages, and without web pages there was no Internet.

7. Script Development: knowing how to make scripts can benefit any company's productivity.

Back to Python

Out of all the possible program developments, Python is a very dynamic programming language that is often used in script, while also capable of being compiled into executable programs (I.E. data files that are locked from normal reading because of their code is rewritten).

Named after the British Comedy *Monty Python's Flying Circus* Guido von Rossum created it back in 1990. Now, Python is written and developed by a team of volunteers and is easily accesable through the Python Software Foundation. In September of 2006, Python released its most updated version, Python 2.5.

There are other versions of Python such as the Java based version Jython which is used to work with a Java coded program. .Net and Mono platforms work with the Iron Python which is a C# version of Python. With the C# version, programmers are given access to all of Python's power and flexibility.

Using both Python and Java work with a substantial library of preowritten code as well as object-oriented that allows it to run on almost any operating system. Python programs are usually complied at the time that the program is running, so that the interpreter reads the program. There is however a way for the program to be compiled into a readable machine code. Additionally, Python does not need an intermediary step in order to perform independently. The platform independence is in the implementation of the interpreter.

2 WHY LEARN PYTHON

Python is an interactive, interpreted program language (interpreted means it does not need to be compiled before executed, but requires an interpreter to modify the script). Python is also object-oriented (in which it is possible to interact and/or execute multiple programs at once).

Python is one of the easiest and user-friendly program languages around, as it is created to look pretty rather than ugly, explicit instead of vague, and easy to read. It is still complex like other programing languages, but with practice and diligence in the material, it will become simple to use.

If you want to learn how to code, you might as well use a program that is free and simple. It thrives on being as simple as possible, and you can even make a few short-cut commands.

For example, the command for Enumerate (which can return an enumerate object like a list) is:

i = 0

for item in iterable:

   print i, item

   i += 1

An alternative coding option is:

for i, item in enumerate(iterable):

   print i, item

And Emulate can even take on a second argument like so:

>>> list(enumerate('abc'))

4

```
[(0, 'a'), (1, 'b'), (2, 'c')]


>>> list(enumerate('abc', 1))

[(1, 'a'), (2, 'b'), (3, 'c')]
```

Python is also easy to learn. The overall structure of Python is fairly clear and easy for those that are new to programming to master. Being that Python runs off a high level language, it strings copies together in a very clear and easy syntax that just uses a few commands.

While mastering the use of Python, one can notice that you'll be able to code some of the more complicated scripts that usually take hours or minutes to program. Within the scripting languages of Python, there are targets that make programming variants fast and easy. This way, should you want to create scripts that simplify everyday work, Python is the program of choice.

While it may not be important, it is a great asset if the scripting languages are easy to read. For example, if you happen to be running off the perl scripting languages, the code can look a lot like hieroglyphics. However Python can descramble the code and make it t where it is more likely for you to remember what your source code does.

Python has a large set of modules that can help you with just about anything you need when it comes to language. The downside to this is that you need to elaborate in order to fully be able to discover the ins and outs of some of the more complex modules.

The biggest thing that makes Python so great is that it can e cross platform. What makes this so useful is that several operating systems are usually used when working. Python is able to run on any machine and therefore you can run whatever scripts you decide to create almost everywhere.

However, Python can also cross platform with ones like Qt or GUIs. This can result in any GUIs that you create not having to be readjusting the source code each time you switch to a new machine.

3 GETTING STARTED WITH INSTALLATION

Windows Version

First, download the latest version of Python 2.7 from the official Website. To be sure you get the fully up-to-date version, click the Downloads > Windows link from the home page of the Python.org web site.

An MSI package is provided with the Windows download. To install it manually, just double-click the file. The MSI package format allows Windows administrators to automate installation with their standard tools.

By design, Python installs to a directory with the version number embedded. For example, Python version 2.7 will install at C:\Python27\. You can download old or new versions of Python, and never have to worry about version conflicts. Of course, only one interpreter can be the default application for Python file types. It also does not automatically modify the environment variable of **path**, or location to the computer file or webpage, so that you always have control over which copy of Python is run.

If typing the full path name for a Python interpreter every time feels tedious, don't worry; you can add the directories for your default Python version to the **PATH**. So if your Python installation is in C:\Python27\, then you can add this to your **PATH**:

C:\Python27\;C:\Python27\Scripts\

You can do this easily by running the following in powershell:

[Environment]::SetEnvironmentVariable("Path", "$env:Path;C:\Python27\;C:\Python27\Scripts\", "User")

The second directory script receives command files when certain packages are installed, so this addition helps a lot. You do not need to install or configure anything else to use Python. But even so, it is strongly recommended that you install the tools and libraries described in the next section before you start building Python applications for real-world use. In particular, you should always install the Setuptools software, as it makes it much easier for you to use other third-party Python libraries.

Mac OS X version

Luckily for Mac, you do not need to install or configure anything else to use Python. Having said that, it is strongly recommended that you install the tools and libraries like the Windows version. We will cover what exactly you'll need before the chapter is over.

The version of Python that ships with OS X is great for learning but it's not good for development. That's due to this version being out of date with the official and current release of Python.

Before installing the up-to date version, you'll need to install GCC. GCC can be obtained by downloading Xcode, the smaller Command Line Tools (which requires an Apple account) or the even smaller OSX-GCC-Installer package.

Note: if you already have Xcode installed, do not install OSX-GCC-Installer. The two programs together may cause conflicting problems to your computer.

Also, if you perform a fresh install of Xcode, you will need to add the commandline tools by running xcode-select --install on the terminal.

While OS X comes with a large number of UNIX utilities, those familiar with Linux systems will notice one key component missing: a decent package manager. You can fix this by installing

Homebrew. Open a Python Terminal or your favorite OSX terminal emulator and run the bolded command in its entirety:

$/usr/bin/ruby-e"$(curl-fsSL
https://raw.githubusercontent.com/Homebrew/install/
master/install)"

The script will explain what changes it will make and prompt you before the installation begins. Once installed, insert your new Homebrew directory at the top of your **PATH** environment variable. You can do this with the following command: **export PATH=/usr/local/bin:/usr/local/sbin:$PATH**

Now, we can install Python 2.7 with this command: **$ brew install python** and you should have everything set in a few minutes.

Linux Version

Python 2.7 comes in many of the latest versions of Linux (CentOS, Fedora, Redhat Enterprise, Ubuntu)

You can double check what Python version you have with the command   script:
$ python --version

Older versions of RHEL and CentOS may come with Python 2.4 instead. Fortunately, there are Extra Packages for Enterprise Linux from their website that can be downloaded.

Setuptools + Pip

Setuptools extends the packaging and installation facilities provided by the distutils in the standard library, and is one of the most important third-party tools for Python. Once you add in Setuptools, you can download and install any compliant Python software product with a single command. It also enables you to add this network installation capability to your own Python software with very little work.

You can find the latest version of Setuptools for Windows by running the Python script here: **ez_setup.py.** You will then have a new command available to use: **easy_install**. But since many criticize the use of this and that it is bad, use the command **pip** instead. Pip allows for uninstallation of packages, and is actively maintained, unlike easy_install. Finally, install Pip with the following Python script: **get-pip.py.** This method also helps in installing with Mac OS X computers.

Pip is automatically installed in Linux centric Python programs 2.7.9 and beyond and 3.4 and beyond. To make sure if Pip is installed, run on the command script: **$ command -v pip**.

Virtual Environments

A Virtual Environment is a tool to keep the dependencies required by different projects in separate places. This is done by creating virtual Python environments for them. This way you do not have to worry about problems like"Project X depends on version 1.x but, Project Y needs 4.x", and can keep your global site-packages directory clean.

4 STARTING TECHNIQUES

When you first open up Python, it should look something like this:

```
7% 20042010 - next - Dictionaries - C:\Users\gunna\Documents\Programming\Python test saves\20042...
 File  Edit  Format  Run  Options  Windows  Help
  File "<pyshell#54>", line 1, in <module>
    print newList.index(9)
ValueError: list.index(x): x not in list
>>> print lew(aList)

Traceback (most recent call last):
  File "<pyshell#55>", line 1, in <module>
    print lew(aList)
NameError: name 'lew' is not defined
>>> print len(aList)
1
>>> print len(newList)
4
>>> print newList
[42, 1, 2, 7]
>>> print aList
[42]
>>> aTuple = (1,3,5)
>>> print aTuple[1] # use indexing like a list
3
>>> aTuple[2] = 7 # error can't change a tuple's elements

Traceback (most recent call last):
  File "<pyshell#62>", line 1, in <module>
    aTuple[2] = 7 # error can't change a tuple's elements
TypeError: 'tuple' object does not support item assignment
>>> tup1 = (1,2,3)
>>> tup2 = tup1 + (4,) #Comme to make it a tuple rather than integer
>>> print tup2
(1, 2, 3, 4)
>>> print tup1
(1, 2, 3)
>>> tup1 = tup1 + (4,)
>>> print tup1
(1, 2, 3, 4)
>>>
                                                          Ln: 1 Col: 0
```

The first step to programming on Python is having it type back the words you send to it. The ">>>" you see is what the program directs you to type for your codes and commands. When you type "print Hello World, SLUAST" for example, it'll come back as this in blue font:

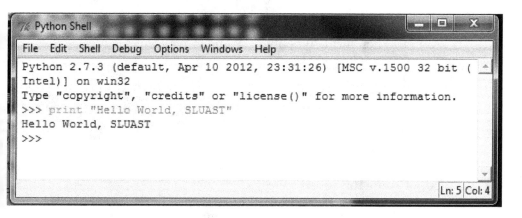

It always helps to know the basics, such as knowing that whatever you print can be send back to you.

The cool thing is that Python can also act as your calculator. When you "print 5", you will just get the number. But if you enter "print 5 + 22", you can expect to see "27" as the response.

Now let's take it a step further and enter a word phrase with strings and numbers. When you "print "im elite,"+1337", you'll actually get an error like so:

Traceback (most recent call last):

File "<pyshell#6>", line 1, in <module>

print "im elite"+1337

TypeError: cannot concatenate 'str' and 'int' objects

The part that begins with "File" says which file, and where in the file the error is located. Then it will show the code, and a little brief description on the error. This is an error where you cannot add strings to integers (only numbers).

Luckily coding with language programs is flexible; you just have to solve around it like the other programmers do. To solve this particular error, you can turn the user you want to use into a variable. Like with regular math, X is a placeholder, so let's make "X = 1337". Then print "im elite" + X and enter.

Except not yet. Otherwise you get the same error.

That's because we haven't changed the variable X's number (1337) into a string by connecting quotation marks (") and apostrophes (') together like this:

X = '1337' (note the apostrophes)

print "im elite "+X (note the quotation marks)

The result will finally read:
im elite 1337 (note the no error!)

Dict/Set comprehensions

You might know about list comprehensions but you might not be aware of dict/set comprehensions. They are simple to use and just as effective. Here is an example:

```
my_dict = {i: i * i for i in xrange(100)}
my_set = {i * 15 for i in xrange(100)}
```

```
# There is only a difference of ':' in both
```

Forcing Float Division

Back to the mathematics, you can divide numbers using the backslash key (/). Normally, division will always give out whole number answers. Normally for Python 2, you have to do something like:

```
result = 1.0/2
```

But there's a handy trick you can do instead to forgo the .0 right here:

```
from __future__ import division
result = ½
# print(result)
# 0.5
```

Of course, you don't have to worry about this if using Python 3 as it is handled by default.

5 IMPORTANT TECHNIQUES AND STRATEGIES

Four types of quotes

Python allows you to put both double quotations as well as single quotes. This is particularly helpful if you are coming from another language because everyone puts a double or single quote for different things. The only thing is that Python does not allow you to interchange the quotes, if you start with one, you must end with the same one. Python also enables you to be able to put two or more types of quotes. Quotes like a triple quote are created by typing three single quotes. A triple-double quote is created by typing three double quotes. Having this function enables the programmer to be able to have several layers of quotes without the worry of escaping their quotes.

Example: print """"I wish that I'd never heard him say, "'She said, "He said, 'Give me five dollars'""""""

The truthfulness of various objects

Unlike if you use Java Python is false if empty and true if not. Definition, you don't have to check to see if the length of a string, list, tuple, or dict is zero or is equal to an empty one. Just checking the truthfulness is enough. Therefore if you expect the number zero to false, all other numbers are true.

Example: 1my_object = 'Test' # True example
2# my_object = '' # False example
3
4if len(my_object) > 0:
5   print 'my_object is not empty'
6
7if len(my_object): # 0 will evaluate to False
8   print 'my_object is not empty'
9

```
10if my_object != '':
11    print 'my_object is not empty'
12
13if my_object: # an empty string will evaluate to False
14    print 'my_object is not empty'
```

Checking if a string contains substring

With Python, you can also test your list, tuple, or dict by testing the expression *'item in list'* or even by using *'item not in list.'*

```
Example: string = 'Hi there' # True example
2# string = 'Good bye' # False example
3if string.find('Hi') != -1:
4    print 'Success!'
```

Using this makes it cleaner and simpler in order to test what needs to be tested in your script.

How to pretty print a list

The average user of a program does not want to see brackets around everything. Instead, they would like to see a clean printed list, even if it is obvious what is in the list. The solution for this is to use a string's 'join' method

```
Example: 1recent_presidents = ['George Bush', 'Bill Clinton',
'George                    W.                    Bush']
2print 'The three most recent presidents were: %s.' % ',
'.join(recent_presidents)
3# prints 'The three most recent presidents were: George
Bush, Bill Clinton, George W. Bush.
```

Using the join method will turn a list into a casting of each item into a string and connecting them with the string that join was called on. The Python program is even smart enough not to put one after the last element.

An added bonus is that Python runs in linear time. Never try and create a string by '+'ing. Instead, list the items together in a for loop. This keeps your list from being ugly, even though it takes more time.

Float division vs integers

Dividing an integer by another will give you a truncated result into an integer. For example, 5/2 will give you the return of 2.

The first way that you can fix this is by turning one of the integers into a float. That way if the values are static, you just append a .0 to make one float. Therefore 5.0/2 will give you 2.5 instead of just 2. Another way you can do this is if you cast one of the values.

The other solution is going to give you a cleaner code, but the biggest thing you must remember is to make sure that your code does not rely on truncation. If you do a from_future_import division while working with Python, you will always get the result of a float while doing division. Just as before 5/2 will give you 2.5. Should you need to truncate the integer somewhere, use the // operation.

```
Example: 15/2      # Returns 2
 25.0/2    # Returns 2.5
 3float(5)/2 # Returns 2.5
 45//2      # Returns 2
 5
 6from __future__ import division
 75/2      # Returns 2.5
 85.0/2    # Returns 2.5
 9float(5)/2 # Returns 2.5
 105//2     # Returns 2
```

Please remember that the point float division will become the default. Should you want your code to future-proof, you will need to use the // operation. If you want the truncating division, you'll need to use the from_future_import divison.

Lambda Functions

While coding, there are times that you want to do a short complex operation multiple times or to pass a function as an argument. In order to do this, you can use the lambda function or you can use your function the normal way. A lambda function is a mini function that will give you the result as a single expression.

Example: 1def add(a,b): return a+b
2
3add2 = lambda a,b: a+b

When using the lambda function, the expression itself can be used within another statement. For example, if you use the map function, a function will be called on every element in your list and therefore will result in giving you the results of the list.

Example: 1squares = map(lambda a: a*a, [1,2,3,4,5])
2# squares is now [1,4,9,16,25]

If you don't use lambda then you will result in having to define each of your functions separately. Using lambda saves a line of code and the variable name.

Syntax for lambda functions. Variables are defines as a comma separated list of variables that your function can receive. Therefore, you are unable to use keywords and you will not want to put these in parentheses. Expressions are defined as an inline python expression. Expressions are what the function returns.

Mapping the list

If you are attempting to square everything in your list, your list may look a little something like this

```
1numbers = [1,2,3,4,5]
2squares = []
3for number in numbers:
4   squares.append(number*number)
5# Now, squares should have [1,4,9,16,25]
```

In doing this, you have "mapped" from one list to another, but, you can also use the map function so that your code looks like this

```
1numbers = [1,2,3,4,5]
2squares = map(lambda x: x*x, numbers)
3# Now, squares should have [1,4,9,16,25]
```

Effectively, you have done the same thing, but made your code shorter. This makes it harder to tell what the map function is when you glance at it. But, it does accept the function and applies it to the list as well as every element in the list. But, the mapping still looks messy. A way to make your list look cleaner is to use a list comprehension. If you do, your list will look a little something like this

```
1numbers = [1,2,3,4,5]
2squares = [number*number for number in numbers]
3# Now, squares should have [1,4,9,16,25]
```

Doing this does the exact same thing as the first two examples, but the biggest difference is that your code is shorter as well as cleaner. This will help make it to where no one has any problem in determining what it does, no matter if they know how Python works or not.

Filtering your list

You've got your list done, and now you want to filter the list. For example, what if you want to remove every element with a value that is equal to or greater than 4? Someone who is new to Python might write their code out like this

```
1numbers = [1,2,3,4,5]
2numbers_under_4 = []
3for number in numbers:
4   if number < 4:
5       numbers_under_4.append(number)
6# Now, numbers_under_4 contains [1,4,9]
```

The code looks simple enough, but it is too long when it could be shortened. Writing the code out this way took four lines, appended to do something completely trivial, and took two degrees of nesting. In order to reduce the size of the code, you need to use the filter function. Using this function will make your code look like this

```
1numbers = [1,2,3,4,5]
2numbers_under_4 = filter(lambda x: x < 4, numbers)
3# Now, numbers_under_4 contains [1,2,3]
```

Just like the map function, the filter function reduces the code size but makes the code look rather ugly. Because the map and filter functions are similar, you can use the list comprehension function so that every element in your list is evaluated and make the code look prettier just as we did with the mapping function. In doing this, your code will look something like this

```
1numbers = [1,2,3,4,5]
2numbers_under_4 = [number for number in numbers if number < 4]
3# Now, numbers_under_4 contains [1,2,3]
```

Now, we have code that is short, clean, and easy to understand.

Mapping and filtering at once

Hopefully by now you understand the concept of how to use the list comprehension function. Ultimately, this has hopefully convinced you that using the map and filter functions are nothing but a waste of your time.

You are able to use the map and filer functions at the same time. This will give you the square of each element that is in your list as well as any element that is under the equivalence of four. Someone new to coding would probably write their code out to look something like this

```
1numbers = [1,2,3,4,5]
2squares = []
3for number in numbers:
4    if number < 4:
5        squares.append(number*number)
6# squares is now [1,4,9]
```

The good thing about this code is that instead of being horizontal, it is beginning to look more and more vertical. But, we still want our code to be simplified. This is where we would attempt to use the map and filter functions. In doing this, your code could come out looking something like this

```
1numbers = [1,2,3,4,5]
2squares = map(lambda x: x*x, filter(lambda x: x < 4, numbers))
3# squares is now [1,4,9]
```

Just as before, our code looks ugly and therefore is unreadable. So, let's try that list comprehension that we've been doing.

```
1numbers = [1,2,3,4,5]
2squares = [number*number for number in numbers if number < 4]
3# square is now [1,4,9]
```

Using the list comprehension has once again made the code readable and shorter as well as cleaner looking. It is better than using the map and filter functions.

List comprehension filters and then maps your list for you to give you a cleaner look and it also cuts out the functions that will ultimately have you using the list comprehension function anyways.

So, why not just do things the easy way and just go straight to using the list comprehension function in order to make your list look clean, short, and readable; even to those who are unsure or even new to using Python.

Generator Expressions

While list comprehensions make things easier while coding, they also have their downside as well. The biggest downside is that list comprehension stores the entire list in the memory at once. While working with smaller lists, this isn't such a problem. It's not even a problem if you have several small lists. But, eventually you'll be making more work for yourself and therefore your method will be pretty inefficient.

The newest function in Python 2.4 is the generator expressions. The best thing about the generator expressions is that it does not load the entire list into the memory at once. Instead, the generator will create what is known as a generator object so that only one element in the list is loaded at a time.

Unfortunately, if you need the entire list for something, using a generator will not be the best option. On the other hand, if you are just passing your list off to something that will take any iterable object, then you can just use the generator function.

Most generator expressions use the same syntax as the list comprehensions but use parentheses instead of brackets. This is what a generated expression code would look like

```
1numbers = (1,2,3,4,5) # Since we're going for efficiency, I'm using a tuple instead of a list ;)
2squares_under_10 = (number*number for number in numbers if number*number < 10)
3# squares_under_10 is now a generator object, from which each successive value can be gotten by calling .next()
4
5for square in squares_under_10:
6   print square,
7# prints '1 4 9'
```

A generated expression is more efficient than using a list comprehension.

If you want to use the generated expressions for a large number of items, you'll only be able to see one item on the list at a time. In the case that you need the entire list at once, you'll need to use the list comprehensions function. Unless your list is too big, using the generator expressions is a good option to use. Otherwise, you're not really going to see any difference in the efficiency.

Generator expressions only use one set of parentheses. While calling a function with only the generator function, you will need to use parentheses. That would look something like this: some_function(item for item in list).

Nested 'for' statements

You can create rather complex lists if you use the list comprehension and generator expressions. But, you will not only be able to map ad filter, you will also be able to nest the for expressions. Once again, someone new to Python might write their code out like this

```
1for x in (0,1,2,3):
2   for y in (0,1,2,3):
3      if x < y:
4         print (x, y, x*y),
5
6# prints (0, 1, 0) (0, 2, 0) (0, 3, 0) (1, 2, 2) (1, 3, 3) (2, 3, 6)
```

Much like a lot of our codes that we've given you examples of, this code is messy and hard to understand. Using the list comprehension function you can take your code from that, to this

```
1print [(x, y, x * y) for x in (0,1,2,3) for y in (0,1,2,3) if x < y]
2# prints [(0, 1, 0), (0, 2, 0), (0, 3, 0), (1, 2, 2), (1, 3, 3), (2, 3, 6)]
```

This code iterates over four values of y and each value over the four values of x and then filters and maps it. Each item on the list is a list of x, y, x * y.

Notice that the xrange (4) has a lot cleaner of a look than the one that uses (0, 1, 2, 3).

Syntax for List Comprehensions and Generator Expressions

A list is defined as any series of items.
Variables are defined as variables that are assigned to the current list elements, very similar to the regular for loop.
Condition is defined as an inline python expression. This includes the local scope and variables. If it is evaluated as true, it will be included in the result.
Element is defined as another inline Python expression but includes the local scope and variables. The actual element will be included in the result.
Reducing a list

While list comprehension is great, you cannot write your entire program using it. Well, in all honesty, you could, but the list comprehension function will not allow you to reduce a list. Reducing a list is to apply a function to the list's first two elements and then ultimately it will move down the list until a single value is reached. For example, should you want to find the product of all the values in your list, you can make a for loop in which your code would look like this

```
1numbers = [1,2,3,4,5]
2result = 1
3for number in numbers:
4    result *= number
5# result is now 120
```

Or, you can even use the reduce function that is built into Python. In that case, your code will look something like this

```
1numbers = [1,2,3,4,5]
2result = reduce(lambda a,b: a*b, numbers)
3# result is now 120
```

Sadly, your list will not be as pretty as it would have been had you use the list comprehension, but, your list will be shorter and sometimes that is just worth the appearance.

Iterating a list: range, range, and enumerate

You can relate the knowledge you used when programming in C. The for loops counted through the index numbers and not the elements. This behavior can be replicated in Python only you'll be using the range or xrange instead of loop. As you pass a value to the range, it will give you a list of integers from 0 all the way to the value of -1. In other words, you will get the index values of a list with that length. The xrange does the same thing, except maybe a bit more efficiently because it doesn't load the entire list into the memory at once.

```
Example: 1strings = ['a', 'b', 'c', 'd', 'e']
2for index in xrange(len(strings)):
```

```
3   print index,
4# prints '0 1 2 3 4'
```

Unfortunately, this is where you usually end up needing to list the elements anyways. The use of having index values is because Python has a function built in called enumerate that helps gives you both the enumerate-ing and the will return an iterator of indexed value pairs. This is what it would look like:

```
1strings = ['a', 'b', 'c', 'd', 'e']
2for index, string in enumerate(strings):
3   print index, string,
4# prints '0 a 1 b 2 c 3 d 4 e'
```

An added advantage to enumerate is that it is cleaner and more readable than the xrang(len()). Therefore, xrange and range are really only useful if you are creating a list of values from scratch.

Checking the condition on any or every list element

If you want to check if any element in your list satisfies a condition, your code would look like this before Python 2.5 came out.

```
1numbers = [1,10,100,1000,10000]
2if [number for number in numbers if number < 10]:
3   print 'At least one element is over 10'
4# Output: 'At least one element is over 10'
```

If the result comes back that none of the elements satisfy the condition you set forth, list comprehension will return a false evaluation. Even so, if you have a non-empty list, it will create an evaluation as true. But, strictly speaking, you do not need to evaluate everything on your list; you can stop if the first element on the list satisfies the condition. While this method may be less than efficient, it could possibly be your only choice if you can't commit to only using Python 2.5 as well as if you need to squeeze all the logic into one expression.

Also, with the new function that is built into Python 2.5, you will be able to do the same thing, only more cleanly and efficiently. Any is smart enough to return and bail true after the first element on the list satisfies your condition. In this example, a generator expression that returned the true or false value on each element in the list. The generator expression can only compute the values as they are needed, and any requests the values as needed.

```
1numbers = [1,10,100,1000,10000]
2if any(number < 10 for number in numbers):
3   print 'Success'
4# Output: 'Success!'
```

If you do want to check every element to make sure that it satisfies the condition, you can. If you do not use Python 2.5, then your code could end up looking like this.

```
1numbers = [1,2,3,4,5,6,7,8,9]
2if len(numbers) == len([number for number in numbers if number < 10]):
3   print 'Success!'
4# Output: 'Success!'
```

Combining multiple lists, item by item

There is a built in function called zip that zips a list together. Once it does that, it returns a list of tuples in which the nth tuple contains the nth item on each of the passed lists.

```
Example: 1letters = ['a', 'b', 'c']
2numbers = [1, 2, 3]
3squares = [1, 4, 9]
4
```

```
5zipped_list = zip(letters, numbers, squares)
6# zipped_list contains [('a', 1, 1), ('b', 2, 4), ('c', 3, 9)]
```

When doing this, you'll see these as the iterator a for loop, as it pulls three values at once

Example: ('for letter, number, squares in zipped_list').

More list operators

Max: the return of the largest element on the list

Min: the return of the smallest element on the list

Sum: the return of all the elements on the list

Advanced logic with sets

Sets differ from lists because they enforce uniqueness while they can't contain more than one of the same items and is unordered. A set also supports a myriad of different logical operations.

In order to make your list unique, you can convert it into a set while simultaneously checking the length at the same time.

```
Example: 1numbers = [1,2,3,3,4,1]
2set(numbers)
3# returns set([1,2,3,4])
4
5if len(numbers) == len(set(numbers)):
6   print 'List is unique!'
7# In this case, doesn't print anything
```

From here, you can convert your set back into a list, but remember that your order was not preserved in the conversion. If you want more information on the different operations that a set can support, you can go to the Python website and check out the Python documents.

Constructing Dictionaries with Keyword Arguments

As you begin to learn Python, you may have missed the alternate ways that you can create a dictionary. In creating keyword arguments, you can pass them directly into the dict constructor where the newly created dictionary will be before returning. Unfortunately, you will be limited to the keys that can be made into your keyword arguments. They have to be valid Python variable names.

Example: 1dict(a=1, b=2, c=3)
2# returns {'a': 1, 'b': 2, 'c': 3}

This option may be a little bit cleaner than a 'regular' dictionary creation, but that depends on your code.

Dicts to list

You've got your dictionary and you know how to make a list, but how do you get the dictionary into a list or even into an iterator? In order to this, you can use the .keys() on the dictionary in order to get a list of keys, or even use the .iterkeys() to get an iterator for the dictionary. On the other hand, you can also use .values() or .intervalues() in order to get a list or iterator of the values for the dictionary. Just remember, that dics are unordered therefore your values won't be in any meaningful order.

In order to preserve both your keys and values, you can turn a dict into a list or iterator of 2 item tuples by using the .items() or the .iteritems() keys.

Example: 1dictionary = {'a': 1, 'b': 2, 'c': 3}
2dict_as_list = dictionary.items()
3#dict_as_list now contains [('a', 1), ('b', 2), ('c', 3)]

Lists to Dicts

Alternatively, you can reverse the process and turn a list of two elements or tuples into a dict

Example: 1dict_as_list = [['a', 1], ['b', 2], ['c', 3]]
2dictionary = dict(dict_as_list)
3# dictionary now contains {'a': 1, 'b': 2, 'c': 3}

Another way to do this is to also use the keywords argument method and create a dictionary.

Example: 1dict_as_list = [['a', 1], ['b', 2], ['c', 3]]
2dictionary = dict(dict_as_list, d=4, e=5)
3# dictionary now contains {'a': 1, 'b': 2, 'c': 3, 'd': 4, 'e': 5}

Being able to convert a list into a dict can come in handy when programming, you just have to find the right program that will support a dict.

Dictionary Comprehensions

Python does not have any built in dictionary comprehensions; you can have something pretty close with a small amount of mess or coding. Use the function .iteritems() in order to turn the dict that you're working on into a list before you throw it into the generator expression (or even the list comprehension) and then cast the list back into a dict.

Example: 1emails = {'Dick': 'bob@example.com', 'Jane': 'jane@example.com', 'Stou': 'stou@example.net'}
2
3email_at_dotcom = dict([name, '.com' in email] for name, email in emails.iteritems())
4
5# email_at_dotcom now is {'Dick': True, 'Jane': True, 'Stou': False}

This is less readable than a straight list comprehension, but however it is better than a loop.

The Right Way

There is a way that you can put select values into the Python 2.5. This new version of Python can support the syntax 'value_if_true if test else value_if_false' therefore, you are able to select a value in one line and not create any weird syntax or even major caveats.

```
1test = True
2# test = False
3result = 'Test is True' if test else 'Test is False'
4# result is now 'Test is True'
```

This bit of coding is messy and a touch unreadable. As another option, you could always chain the multiple tests into one line.

```
1test1 = False
2test2 = True
3result = 'Test1 is True' if test1 else 'Test1 is False, test2 is True' if test2 else 'Test1 and Test2 are both False'
```

To begin with, the if/else is evaluated and then if the test is found false, the second if/else is evaluated. If you so desire to, you can do more complex evaluations, adding in parentheses will help with this should you decide to use them.

If the if/else is new, you will still be able to check out some of the tricks that will be mentioned later on. If you only plan on programming while using Python 2.5, you will still be running into these older codes and using them. If you need backwards compatibility or even don't have the newest version of Python, the tricks below will come in more use than if you are using Python.

The and/or trick

While using Python, the 'and 'or' functions are complex. And-ing two expressions together does not return a true if both are true as well as false if both are a false. The first false value will return as well as if the last value is true with the and function. Otherwise known as, if the first value is a false that is returned, then the last value is returned. The result, as you would have guessed would only happen if both are true, then the last value is returned true and will be evaluated to a true function when tested in a Boolean test. If it is false, then the one returned will be evaluated as false in the Boolean test.

Or-ing the expressions together is similar. 'Or's return only if the first true value or the last true value are false. If both are false, then the last value will be returned false and will evaluate as false in the Boolean test. Same is true if the value is returned true.

Sadly, this will not help you if you are trying to test for truthfulness. But, you can use the 'and' 'or' functions for other purposes while using Python. This will help when you use a ternary conditional assignment operator such as 'test ? value_if_true : value_if_false'

Example: 1test = True
2# test = False
3result = test and 'Test is True' or 'Test is False'
4# result is now 'Test is True'

If a test is true and it is skipped over by the statement, ten it returns the right half as true is true or true is false. The test will continue left to right or until the statement results in the first true value, test is true.

On the other hand, if the test is false and the statement returns the test. The process will continue left to right until the result is test or test is false. If the test is false, then the statement skips over it and returns to the right half as test is false.

You'll need to be careful that the middle (if_true) is never false. Should it be false, then you will have an 'or' statement and it will be skipped over and return the rightmost (if_false) value, it doesn't matter what the test value is.

Using true and false as indexes

You can select values that can be used with the true and false as list indexes and even take advantage of the fact that false==0 and true==1

```
1test = True
2# test = False
3result = ['Test is False','Test is True'][test]
4# result is now 'Test is True'
```

Using this is a more straightforward way than to use the and/or trick and is free of the problem where the value_if_true must be true as well.

This way however suffers from one major flaw. Both lists of items need to be evaluated before truthfulness can be checked. If you are using strings or other simple items, this isn't such a big deal. But, when using it for significant computation or an I/O, you don't want to end up doing twice the work so this way is not recommended. In order to prevent yourself from doing twice the work, you can use the right way in other words you can use the and/or trick.

Please note that the index method only works if you know that the test is false or true. If you do not know, then it is recommended that you write bool(test) instead of test in order to get the same behavior as the and/or trick.

Default argument values are only evaluated once

Example: 1def function(item, stuff = []):
2   stuff.append(item)
3   print stuff
4
5function(1)
6# prints '[1]'
7
8function(2)
9# prints '[1,2]' !!!

The default value for any function argument is only evaluated once if the function is defined. Python assigns this to the value to the correct variable when the function is called.

Python will not check if the value is changed or the location of the memory. Python just assigns it to a value that any caller needs it to be assigned to. So, should the value be changed, the change will persist across all function calls. If you append a value to the list, it will be represented by stuff, and you change the default value then it will be changed for all eternity. If you call functioning once again in order to look for a default value, the modified default will be given to you.

Solution: do not use mutable objects as function defaults. If you do this, you will not be able to modify them. Here is a better example of what should have been written above.

1def function(item, stuff = None):
2   if stuff is None:
3   stuff = []
4   stuff.append(item)
5   print stuff
6
7function(1)
8# prints '[1]'
9

```
10function(2)
11# prints '[2]', as expected
```

None is immutable so that will not be changed, but it also saves you from accidentally changing the value of your default.

A plus side is that an experienced programmer could probably use this trick and effectively create a C-style of 'static variables.

6 GLOSSARY

There are a lot of different commands and options for language programs and Python is no different. A good number will be shown here.

Class

Python supports the object oriented programming paradigm. Much like other OOP languages, Python has different classes that are defined by wireframes of different objects. A class may have subclasses but may only inherit directly from one superclass.

Syntax:

```
class ClassName(object):
    """This is a class"""
    class_variable
    def __init__(self,*args):
        self.args = args
    def __repr__(self):
        return "Something to represent the object as a string"
    def other_method(self,*args):
        # do something else
```

Example:

```
class Horse(object):
    """Horse represents a Horse"""
    species = "Equus ferus caballus"
    def __init__(self,color,weight,wild=False):
        self.color = color
        self.weight = weight
        self.wild = wild
    def __repr__(self):
        return "%s horse weighing %f and wild status is %b" %
(self.color,self.weight,self.wild)
```

```
    def make_sound(self):
        print "neighhhh"
    def movement(self):
        return "walk"
```

Syntax:

```
class ClassName(SuperClass):
    # same as above
    # use 'super' keyword to get from above
```

Example:

```
class RaceHorse(Horse):
    """A faster horse that inherits from Horse"""
    def movement(self):
        return "run"
    def movement_slow(self):
        return super(Horse,self).movement()
    def __repr__(self):
        return "%s race horse weighing %f and wild status is %b"
(self.color,self.weight,self.wild)

>> horse3 = RaceHorse("white",200)
>> print horse3.movement_slow()
"walk"
>> print horse3.movement()
"run"
```

Comments

Single Line Comments: this is augmenting code in which human readable descriptions can help with document design decisions.

Example: # this is a single line comment.

Multi-line Comments: these comments span several lines. You need to use this if you have more than four lines of single comments in a row.

Example:

'''

this is
a multi-line
comment, i am handy for commenting out whole
chunks of code very fast
'''

Dictionaries

These are Python's built-in associative data type. The dictionary is made up of different key-value pairs where each key corresponds with a different value. Much like sets, dictionaries are unordered.

The keys must be immutable and hashable so that the value can be any type. The most common examples of these keys are tuples, numbers, and strings. One single dictionary can contain the key types of varying values and varying types.

Syntax:

```
dict() #creates new empty dictionary
{} #creates new empty dictionary
```

Example:

```
>> my_dict = {}
>> content_of_value1 = "abcd"
>> content_of_value2 = "wxyz"
>> my_dict.update({"key_name1":content_of_value1})
>> my_dict.update({"key_name2":content_of_value2})
>> my_dict
{'key_name1':"abcd", 'key_name2':"wxyz"}
>> my_dict.get("key_name2")
"wxyz"
```

Syntax:

{key1:value1,key2:value2}

Example:

```
>> my_dict = {"key1":[1,2,3],"key2":"I am a string",123:456}
>> my_dict["key1"] #[1,2,3]
>> my_dict[123] #456
>> my_dict["new key"] = "New value"
>> print my_dict
{"key2":"I am a string", "new key":"New value",
"key1":[1,2,3],123:456}
```

Functions

These functions can be used as abstract pieces of code that can be used elsewhere.

Syntax

```
def function_name(parameters):
  # Some code here
```

Example

```
def add_two(a, b):
  c = a + b
  return c

# or without the interim assignment to c
def add_two(a, b):
  return a + b
```

Syntax

```
def function_name(parameters,
named_default_parameter=value):
  # Some code here
```

Example

```
def shout(exclamation="Hey!"):
  print exclamation

shout() # Displays "Hey!"

shout("Watch Out!") # Displays "Watch Out!"
```

Function Objects

These are first class objects. This means that they can be stored in lists or variables and even can be returned by other functions.

Example

```
# Storing function objects in variables:

def say_hello(name):
  return "Hello, " + name

foo = say_hello("Alice")
# Now the value of 'foo' is "Hello, Alice"

fun = say_hello
# Now the value of 'fun' is a function object we can use like
the original function:
bar = fun("Bob")
# Now the value of 'bar' is "Hello, Bob"
```

Example

```
# Returning functions from functions

# A simple function
def say_hello(greeter, greeted):
  return "Hello, " + greeted + ", I'm " + greeter + "."
```

```
# We can use it like this:
print say_hello("Alice", "Bob") # Displays "Hello, Bob, I'm
Alice."

# We can also use it in a function:
def produce_greeting_from_alice(greeted):
  return say_hello("Alice", greeted)

print produce_greeting_from_alice("Bob") # Displays
"Hello, Bob, I'm Alice."

# We can also return a function from a function by nesting
them:
def produce_greeting_from(greeter):
  def greet(greeted):
    return say_hello(greeter, greeted)
  return greet

# Here we create a greeting function for Eve:
produce_greeting_from_eve =
produce_greeting_from("Eve")
# 'produce_greeting_from_eve' is now a function:
print produce_greeting_from_eve("Alice") # Displays
"Hello, Alice, I'm Eve."

# You can also invoke the function directly if you want:
print produce_greeting_from("Bob")("Eve") # Displays
"Hello, Eve, I'm Bob."
```

Example

```
# Using functions in a dictionary instead of long if
statements:

# Let's say we have a variable called 'current_action' and we
want stuff to happen based on its value:

if current_action == 'PAUSE':
```

```
  pause()
elif current_action == 'RESTART':
  restart()
elif current_action == 'RESUME':
  resume()

# This can get long and complicated if there are many values.
# Instead, we can use a dictionary:

response_dict = {
  'PAUSE': pause,
  'RESTART': restart,
  'RESUME': resume
}

response_dict[current_action]() # Gets the correct function
from response_dict and calls it
```

len()

if you use len(some object) it will usually return the number of top-level items that are being queried.

Syntax

len(iterable)

Example

```
>> my_list = [0,4,5,2,3,4,5]
>> len(my_list)
7

>> my_string = 'abcdef'
>> len(my_string)
6
```

List Comprehensions

This is a convenient way to generate or extract information from a list that you create

Syntax

[variable for variable in iterable condition]
[variable for variable in iterable]

Example

```
>> x_list = [1,2,3,4,5,6,7]
>> even_list = [num for num in x_list if (num % 2 == 0)]
>> even_list
[2,4,6]

>> m_list = ['AB', 'AC', 'DA', 'FG', 'LB']
>> A_list = [duo for duo in m_list if ('A' in duo)]
>> A_list
['AB', 'AC', 'DA']
```

Lists

This is a data type that orders and holds a collection of values. This can be any type of values. Lists in Python are orders of mutable data types. Unlike tuples, lists are able to be modified in place or in other words, as you create them.

Example

```
>> x = [1, 2, 3, 4]
>> y = ['spam', 'eggs']
>> x
[1, 2, 3, 4]
>> y
['spam','eggs']
```

```
>> y.append('mash')
>> y
['spam', 'eggs', 'mash']

>> y += ['beans']
>> y
['spam', 'eggs', 'mash', 'beans']
```

Loops

For Loops:

These are clean iteration syntax. The colon and the indentation are usually indicators of for loops.

Example

```
>> for i in range(0, 3):
>>    print(i*2)
0
2
4

>> m_list = ["Sir", "Lancelot", "Coconuts"]
>> for item in m_list:
>>    print(item)
Sir
Lancelot
Coconuts
>> w_string = "Swift"
>> for letter in w_string:
>>    print(letter)
S
w
i
f
t
```

While Loops:

These are permits codes execute repeatedly until a certain condition is met. Usually this is only useful if the number of iterations required is unknown prior to flow entering the loop.

Syntax

```
while condition:
    //do something
```

Example

```
>> looping_needed = True
>>
>> while looping_needed:
>>    # some operation on data
>>    if condition:
>>        looping_needed = False
```

Print()

This function displays the output of a program. It is arguably more consistent when you're using the parenthesized version.

Example

```
>> # this will work in all modern versions of Python
>> print("some text here")
"some text here"

>> # but this only works in Python versions lower than 3.x
>> print "some text here too"
"some text here too"
```

Range()

A rang() function is the function that returns the list of integers to the sequence that is defined by arguments passed to it.

Syntax

argument variations:
range(terminal)
range(start, terminal)
range(start, terminal, step_size)

Example

```
>> range(4)
[0, 1, 2, 3]

>> range(2, 8)
[2, 3, 4, 5, 6, 7]

>> range(2, 13, 3)
[2, 5, 8, 11]
```

Sets

A collection of unique and unordered set of items. Some iterables can be converted into sets.

Example

```
>> new_set = {1, 2, 3, 4, 4, 4,'A', 'B', 'B', 'C'}
>> new_set
{'A', 1, 'C', 3, 4, 2, 'B'}

>> dup_list = [1,1,2,2,2,3,4,55,5,5,6,7,8,8]
>> set_from_list = set(dup_list)
>> set_from_list
{1, 2, 3, 4, 5, 6, 7, 8, 55}
```

Slice

This is a Python way of extracting "slices" or pieces of a list by using a special bracket notation which specifies the start and end of the section that you wish to extract. By leaving the beginning value blank, it indicates that you wish to start at the beginning of the list. By leaving the ending value blank, it means that you wish to go to the end of the list. If you use negative value references at the end of the list such as a list of four elements, -1 being the forth element. Slicing can be used as another way to yield yet another list, even if you just extract a single value.

Example

```
>> # Specifying a beginning and end:
>> x = [1, 2, 3, 4]
>> x[2:3]
[3]

>> # Specifying start at the beginning and end at the second
element
>> x[:2]
[1, 2]

>> # Specifying start at the next to last element and go to the
end
>> x[-2:]
[3, 4]

>> # Specifying start at the beginning and go to the next to
last element
>> x[:-1]
[1, 2, 3]

>> # Specifying a step argument returns every n-th item
>> y = [1, 2, 3, 4, 5, 6, 7, 8]
>> y[::2]
[1, 3, 5, 7]
```

```
>> # Return a reversed version of the list ( or string )
>> x[::-1]
[4, 3, 2, 1]

>> # String reverse
>> my_string = "Aloha"
>> my_string[::-1]
"aholA"
```

Str()

Using this function will allow you to represent the content in which the variable is shown as a string. It provides the data type that the variable provides, but in a neat way. Str() cannot change the variable in place, instead it just returns it to the 'stringified' version of it. In more technical terms, str() calls a special _str_ method if an object is passed to it.

Syntax

str(object)

Example

```
>> # such features can be useful for concatenating strings
>> my_var = 123
>> my_var
123

>> str(my_var)
'123'

>> my_booking = "DB Airlines Flight " + str(my_var)
>> my_booking
'DB Airlines Flight 123'
```

Strings

These store characters using more built-in and convent methods. You can modify a strings content but they cannot be changed in place.

Example

```
>> my_string1 = "this is a valid string"
>> my_string2 = 'this is also a valid string'
>> my_string3 = 'this is' + ' ' + 'also' + ' ' + 'a string'
>> my_string3
"this is also a string"
```

Tuples

This is a data type that can hold an ordered collection of values but can be any type of values. The tuples are immutable which mean once they are created, they cannot be changed.

Example

```
>> x = (1, 2, 3, 4)
>> y = ('spam', 'eggs')

>> my_list = [1,2,3,4]
>> my_tuple = tuple(my_list)
>> my_tuple
(1, 2, 3, 4)
```

Tuple Assignment

These can be expanded into variables rather easily.

Example

```
name, age = ("Alice", 19)
# Now name has the value "Alice" and age has the value 19

# You can also omit the parentheses:
name, age = "Alice", 19
```

Variables

Variables are usually assigned to values by using the = operator. This is not to be confused with the == sign that is used for testing equality. A variable can hold any sort of value type such as dictionaries, functions and even lists.

Example

```
>> X = 12
>> X
12
```

7 CONCLUSION

Thank you again for ordering this book!

I hope this book was able to help you to learn how to code with Python.

The next step, in case you haven't done so already, is to apply what you have learned into coding. And from there, the sky's the limit to what you can code and learn.

Finally, if you enjoyed this book, then I'd like to ask you for a favor, would you be kind enough to leave a review for this book on Amazon? It'd be greatly appreciated!

Thank you and good luck

ABOUT THE AUTHOR

Jonathan Bates is the founder of Techtalk books and has been a computer enthusiast for over 20 years. After graduating from the University of East Anglia, Norwich and gaining his masters degree at Imperial College, London in Computer Engineering, Jonathan worked at major technology companies across Asia and the U.S.A. In 2014 he decided to settle back to his native home, London. He now works as a computer programmer and has developed a love for writing articles and books, having discovered that many people don't understand the fundamentals of getting the most out of their software. His passion for programming comes out in his writing, which he is currently in the process of writing a series of programming books

www.ingramcontent.com/pod-product-compliance
Lightning Source LLC
Chambersburg PA
CBHW061041050326
40689CB00012B/2920